I0883277

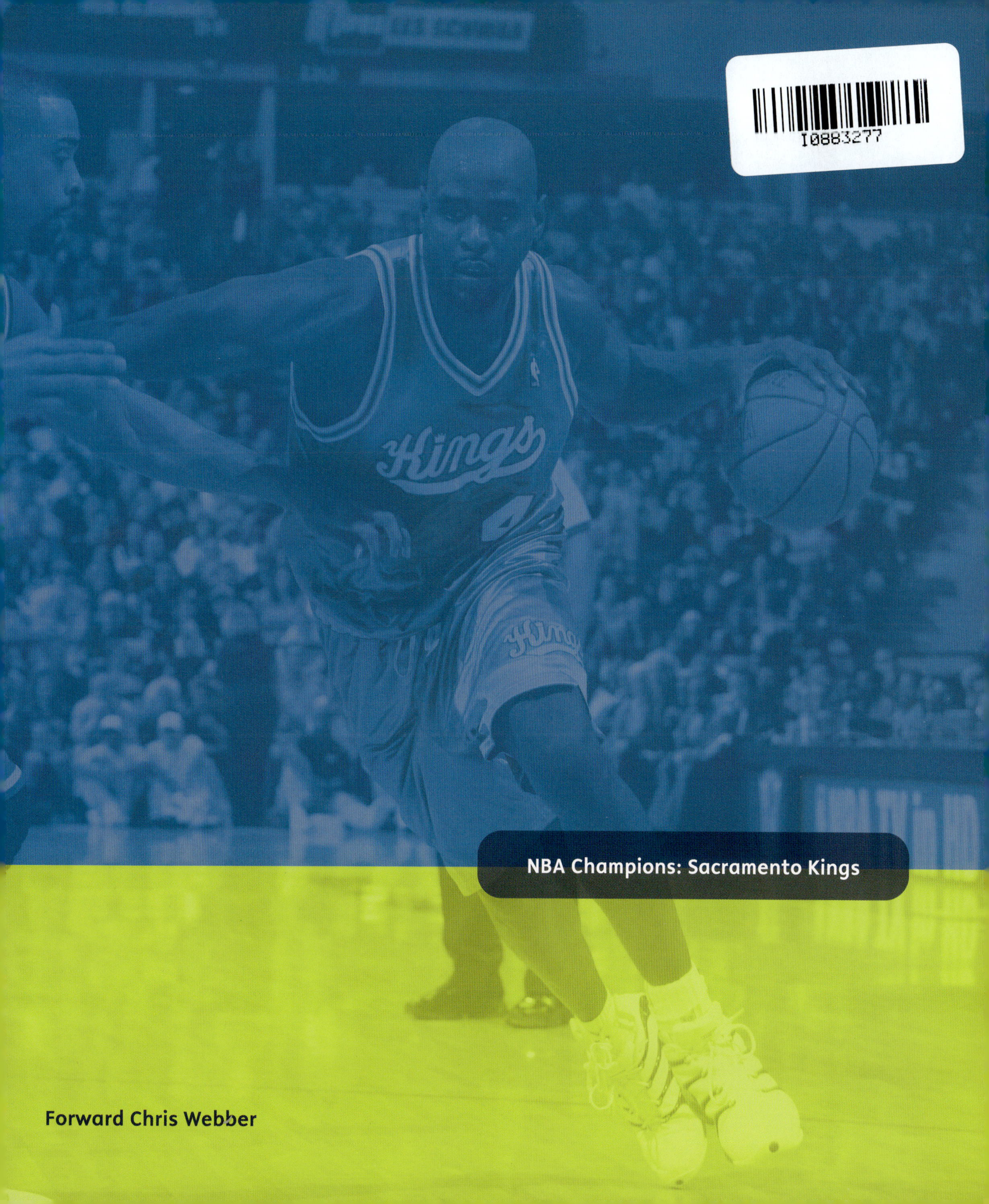

NBA Champions: Sacramento Kings

Forward Chris Webber

Guard Mitch Richmond

NBA CHAMPIONS

SACRAMENTO KINGS

DENNY BULCAO, JR.

CREATIVE EDUCATION / CREATIVE PAPERBACKS

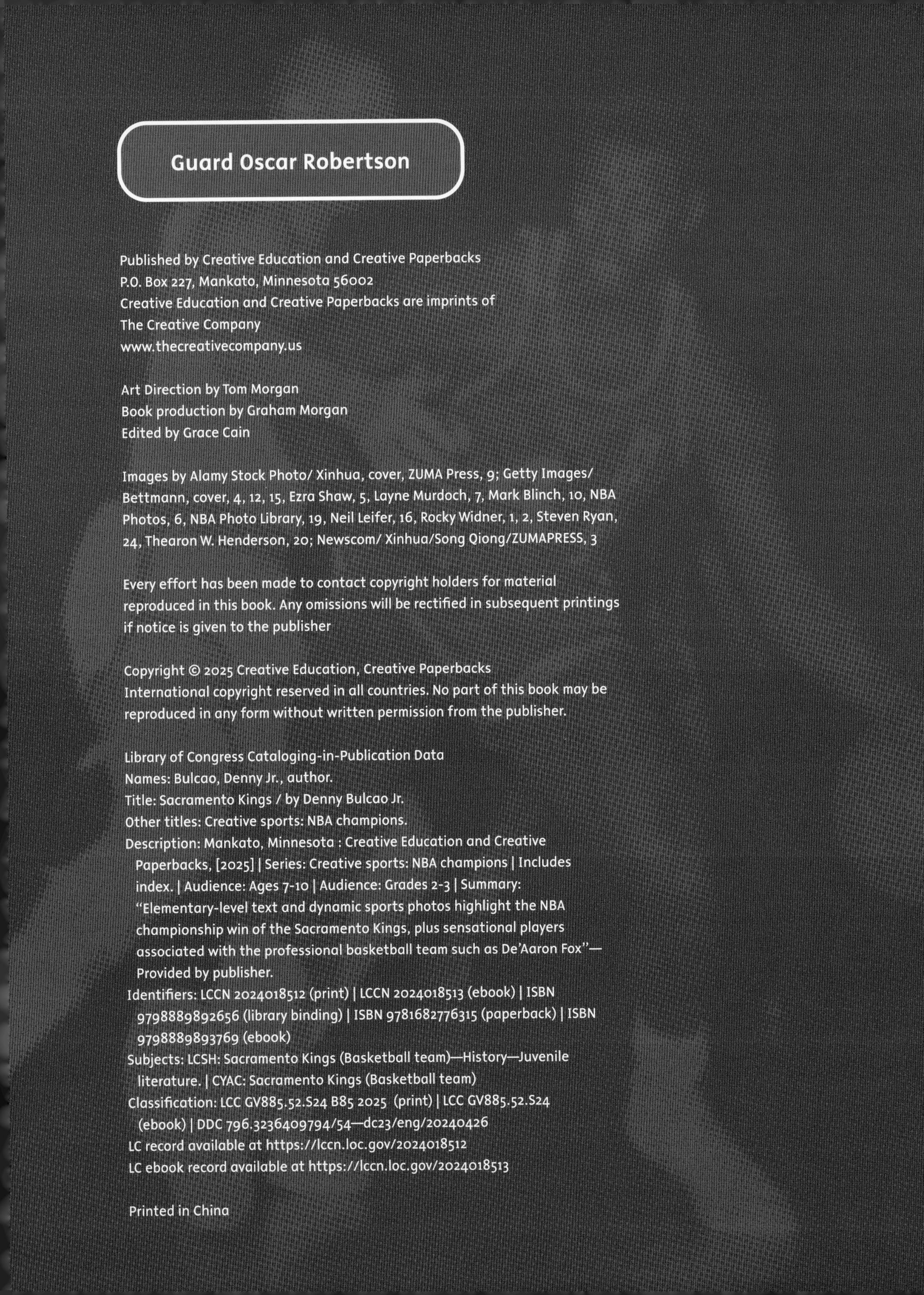

Guard Oscar Robertson

Published by Creative Education and Creative Paperbacks
P.O. Box 227, Mankato, Minnesota 56002
Creative Education and Creative Paperbacks are imprints of
The Creative Company
www.thecreativecompany.us

Art Direction by Tom Morgan
Book production by Graham Morgan
Edited by Grace Cain

Images by Alamy Stock Photo/ Xinhua, cover, ZUMA Press, 9; Getty Images/ Bettmann, cover, 4, 12, 15, Ezra Shaw, 5, Layne Murdoch, 7, Mark Blinch, 10, NBA Photos, 6, NBA Photo Library, 19, Neil Leifer, 16, Rocky Widner, 1, 2, Steven Ryan, 24, Thearon W. Henderson, 20; Newscom/ Xinhua/Song Qiong/ZUMAPRESS, 3

Every effort has been made to contact copyright holders for material reproduced in this book. Any omissions will be rectified in subsequent printings if notice is given to the publisher

Copyright © 2025 Creative Education, Creative Paperbacks
International copyright reserved in all countries. No part of this book may be reproduced in any form without written permission from the publisher.

Library of Congress Cataloging-in-Publication Data
Names: Bulcao, Denny Jr., author.
Title: Sacramento Kings / by Denny Bulcao Jr.
Other titles: Creative sports: NBA champions.
Description: Mankato, Minnesota : Creative Education and Creative Paperbacks, [2025] | Series: Creative sports: NBA champions | Includes index. | Audience: Ages 7-10 | Audience: Grades 2-3 | Summary: "Elementary-level text and dynamic sports photos highlight the NBA championship win of the Sacramento Kings, plus sensational players associated with the professional basketball team such as De'Aaron Fox"—Provided by publisher.
Identifiers: LCCN 2024018512 (print) | LCCN 2024018513 (ebook) | ISBN 9798889892656 (library binding) | ISBN 9781682776315 (paperback) | ISBN 9798889893769 (ebook)
Subjects: LCSH: Sacramento Kings (Basketball team)—History—Juvenile literature. | CYAC: Sacramento Kings (Basketball team)
Classification: LCC GV885.52.S24 B85 2025 (print) | LCC GV885.52.S24 (ebook) | DDC 796.3236409794/54—dc23/eng/20240426
LC record available at https://lccn.loc.gov/2024018512
LC ebook record available at https://lccn.loc.gov/2024018513

Printed in China

Forward Domantas Sabonis

Guard Red Holzman

CONTENTS

Home of the Kings

Sacramento is the capital of California. It is located in the northern part of the state where the Sacramento and American Rivers meet. The city grew quickly when gold was discovered in the area in 1848. Sacramento has an **arena** called Golden 1 Center. It is home to the Kings basketball team.

Golden1
Credit Union
CENTER

Forward Domantas Sabonis

The Kings are part of the National Basketball Association (NBA). They play against other teams in the NBA. They try to win the **NBA Finals**. **Rivals** of the Kings are the Golden State Warriors, Los Angeles Lakers, Los Angeles Clippers, and Phoenix Suns. They are all in the Pacific Division in the Western Conference.

Guard Larry Drew

Naming the Kings

The team got its start in Rochester, New York, in 1945. A teenager won a contest to name the team the Rochester Royals. When the team moved to Kansas City, they found that the city already had a baseball team called the Royals. A king is a royal leader, so "Kings" became the team's new name. They kept the name when they moved to Sacramento.

Kings History

The Rochester Royals reached their first Finals in 1951. Point guard Bob Davies scored key points. They became NBA champions!

In 1957, the Royals moved to Cincinnati, Ohio. A few years later, Oscar Robertson joined the team. He was a great shooter, passer, and rebounder. He led the Cincinnati Royals to the **playoffs** six years in a row.

Guard Oscar Robertson

Guard Nate Archibald

The Royals moved again in 1972. In Missouri, they picked up the Kings name. Their star was speedy guard Nate Archibald. His nickname was "Tiny," but he made big baskets.

The Kings moved to Sacramento in 1985. They started poorly. Then powerful forward-center Chris Webber arrived in 1998. He helped the Kings win 61 games in 2001–02. The Kings almost reached the Finals that year.

Other Kings Stars

Swingman Jack Twyman and power forward Maurice Stokes were childhood friends. They starred together in Rochester and Cincinnati. Sam Lacey was the team's top rebounder for nine seasons. Vlade Divac was a key player for six years. Center DeMarcus Cousins was a terrific scorer and shot blocker.

Swingman Jack Twyman

Guard De'Aaron Fox

In 2017, the Kings made a trade with several players. Cousins left, and high-scoring guard Buddy Hield joined the team. In a later trade, Hield left and Domantas Sabonis joined the team.

Sabonis and De'Aaron Fox are the team's current stars. The team reached the playoffs in the 2022–23 season for the first time in 16 seasons. Fans hope they will win a championship soon.

About the Kings

First season: 1945–46

Conference/division: Western Conference, Pacific Division

Team colors: pure black, royal purple, gray, white, and royal blue

Home arena: Golden 1 Center

NBA CHAMPIONSHIPS:

1951, 4 games to 3 over New York Knicks

TEAM WEBSITE:

https://www.nba.com/kings/

Glossary

arena—a large building with seats for spectators, where sports games and entertainment events are held

NBA Finals—a series of games between two teams at the end of the playoffs; the first team to win four games is the champion

playoffs—games that the best teams play after a regular season to see who the champion will be

rival—a team that plays extra hard against another team

swingman—a basketball player who can play guard or forward

Forward Harrison Barnes

Index